WEEKLY MEAL PLANNER
with
PLANT PARADOX
Quick Reference Guide

ISBN-13: 978-1724076243

INTRODUCTION

This 52-week menu planner is intended as a companion to the Plant Paradox book series by Steven Gundry, M.D. It includes reference materials to help you maintain compliance with the program while planning your weekly meals and grocery shopping.

The information provided here is based on Dr. Gundry's recommended program and has been curated from numerous resources consistent with the principles of eating a reduced-lectin diet for weight loss and optimal health.

The Plant Paradox program is comprised of 3 phases. The lists below are not inclusive of all compliant foods; rather, they are a summary intended to inspire your meal planning. (*A more comprehensive list of compliant foods appears later in this notebook.*) Your approach to the program will be influenced by your unique health needs, the dietary preferences of you and your family, and your ability to adopt the Plant Paradox ideals in a way that fits your lifestyle.

PHASE 1
3 Days

FOCUS ON:
Leafy greens
Cruciferous vegetables:
  Cabbage
  Cauliflower
  Broccoli
  Brussels sprouts
  Kale
Avocados
Wild-caught seafood*
Pastured poultry*

OTHER PHASE 1 FOODS:
Artichokes
Asparagus
Celery
Mushrooms
Radishes
Olives
Onions, leeks, garlic
Compliant nuts (½ cup daily)

* Maximum 4 oz. twice a day

PHASE 2
6 Weeks

ADD TO PHASE 1 FOODS:
Turnips, parsnips, rutabaga
Yams, sweet potatoes
Green plantains
Shirataki (konjac) noodles
Okra
Carrots
Beets
Eggs (pastured or Omega-3)
Chocolate (72%+, 1 oz. daily)

Compliant grains (millet, sorghum)
Compliant dairy (1 oz. daily)
Compliant flours
Compliant sweeteners

PHASE 3
Long-term

REDUCE:
Gradually reduce animal protein to 2-4 oz. daily

ADD*:
Pressure-cooked legumes
Indian white basmati rice
Peeled, de-seeded:
  Tomatoes (or pressure-cooked)
  Peppers (or pressure-cooked)
  Zucchini (or pressure-cooked)
  Cucumber

Grass-fed beef, pork
Local fruit, in season

* Reintroduce high-lectin foods slowly and consume in moderation. Depending upon your health needs, some or all of these Phase 3 additions may not be suitable for your personal long-term diet.

COMPLIANT FOOD LIST

This alphabetical list of Plant Paradox compliant foods is provided as a quick reference tool. This is not the complete 'Yes' list – Dr. Gundry's list of approved foods changes from time to time based on new research and information. This list is compiled from multiple sources based on current information. **Some foods listed here should be eaten in moderation and/or only in Phase 3.** Refer to Dr. Gundry's book series for a thorough explanation and follow him on YouTube to stay up to date.

Algae, algae oil
Almonds (blanched)
   Includes almond flour, & milk
   cheese & yogurt (all unsweetened)
Anchovies
Arrowroot flour
Artichokes
Asparagus
Avocados, plus oil & mayonnaise
Bamboo shoots
Bananas (green)
Beans (organic canned,)*
Beef (grass-fed, grass-finished)
Beets (raw is best)
Bok choy
Brazil nuts
Broccoli
Brussels sprouts
Buffalo mozzarella or butter
Butter (French or Italian)
Cabbage
Cactus (prickly pear, nopales)

Calamari, squid
Carrots (raw is best)
Cassava/yuca, cassava flour
Cauliflower
Celery, celery root/celeriac
Cheese from France, Italy or
   Switzerland, or goat or sheep
Chestnuts, chestnut flour
Chives
Chocolate (dark, 72%+)
Cocoa powder (non-alkalized)
Coconut aminos
Coconut, coconut flour
Coconut milk, cream (unsweetened)
Coconut oil
Cod liver oil
Coffee
Cream (heavy, organic)
Cream cheese (full fat, organic)
Curry paste
Eggs (pastured or Omega-3)
Erythritol (Swerve)

Fennel
Figs (fresh, in-season only)
Fish (wild-caught)
Fish sauce (sugar-free)
Flax seeds
Fruit (fresh, in-season only)
Game (wild or grass-fed/finished)
Garlic
Ghee
Ginger
Goat milk, butter, cheese, kefir
Green banana flour
Hazelnuts, hazelnut flour
Hearts of palm, noodles
Hemp protein powder
Hemp seeds/hearts, milk
Hemp tofu
Herbs
Honey (local or Manuka)
Horseradish
Hot sauce (sriracha, etc.)
Inulin (Just Like Sugar)

Compliant Convenience Foods

Convenience foods can be expensive but keeping some on hand may keep you on track when time is short. Be sure to check the label before you buy. Food manufacturers may change their recipes and introduce non-compliant ingredients. This list is a sampling of what you may find in your grocery store or specialty market.

Barely Bread
Birch Benders Paleo Pancake & Waffle Mix
Bob's Red Mill Egg Replacer
Capello's Fettuccini Noodles
Capello's Lasagna Noodles
Capello's Naked Pizza Crust
Chebe Bread Mix & Garlic-Onion Breadsticks Mix
Chebe Focaccia & Pizza Crust Mix
Flackers – Sea Salt or Rosemary only
Jackson's Honest Sweet Potato Chips
Julian Bakery PaleoThin Wraps
Julian Bakery PaleoThin Coconut Flakes Cereal
Kevita Coconut or Coconut Mojito Kombucha
Kirkland (Costco) Basil Pesto
Lakanto Maple Flavored Syrup

Muir Glen Pizza Sauce
Pomi Pizza Sauce
Pomi Strained Tomatoes
Primal Kitchen salad dressings
Siete Tortillas
Simple Mills Artisan Bread Mix
Simple Mills Pizza Dough Mix
Terra Cassava Chips
Testa's Pasta Sauce and Marinara Sauce
Teton Waters Ranch Grass Fed Beef Sausages
The Real Coconut tortillas/wraps
The Real Coconut Tortilla Chips – Original
The Real Coconut Tortilla Chips – Himalayan Sea Salt
Trader Joe's frozen Cauliflower Gnocchi
Wholly Guacamole – Organic or Classic only

COMPLIANT FOOD LIST, continued

Jackfruit
Jerusalem artichokes (sunchokes)
Jicama
Kale
Kanten pasta
Kefir (goat & sheep)
Kelp noodles
Kimchi
Kohlrabi
Kombucha (low sugar only)
Konjac root (glucomannan)
Lamb (pastured)
Leeks
Lemongrass
Lettuce, all leafy greens
Macadamia nuts, oil
Mango (green)
MCT oil
Milk (A2)(small amounts only)
Milk (goat, hemp)
Millet, millet flour & pasta
Miso
Monk fruit
Mushrooms
Mustard
Nutritional yeast
Okra
Olives, Olive oil (extra virgin)

Onions, shallots, chives, scallions
Palm oil, red palm oil
Papaya (green)
Parsnips
Pecans
Peppers*
Perilla, perilla oil
Persimmon
Pine nuts
Pistachios
Plantains (green)
Pork (pastured)
Potatoes (pressure-cooked only)*
Poultry (pastured)
Proscuitto
Psyllium
Radicchio
Radishes
Rhubarb
Rutabaga
Salmon (wild caught, canned, smoked)
Sardines
Sauerkraut (raw)
Seasonings (except chili flakes)
Seaweed, nori
Sesame seeds, flour, oil
Shellfish (wild-caught)
Shirataki noodles (soy-free)

Sorghum, sorghum flour & pasta
Sour cream (full fat, organic)
Stevia (Truvia, SweetLeaf)
Sweet potatoes, flour, noodles
Tapioca flour/starch
Tahini
Taro root
Tea
Tempeh (grain-free)
Tequila (reposado or añejo)
Tiger nuts, flour
Tomatoes (peeled, de-seeded)*
Tomato paste
Tomato sauce (peeled, de-seeded)*
Tuna (small)(including canned)
Turnips
Vinegar (any; no added sugar)
Walnuts, walnut oil
Wasabi
Water chestnuts
Whey protein powder
Whiskey, scotch (aged in wood)
Wine (sparkling, red)
Xylitol
Yacón
Yams
Yogurt (coconut, goat, sheep)
  (unsweetened)

* Pressure Cooking and the PP Program

Recent research has indicated that beans, peas, potatoes, peppers, tomatoes, squash, and quinoa can be made compliant through pressure-cooking, which destroys the lectins in those foods. The *minimum* pressure-cooking time required to eliminate lectins is 7.5 minutes. It's fine to pressure cook for a longer time if that's what your recipe calls for. All commercially sold canned beans are already pressure-cooked. Dr. Gundry recommends choosing beans that are organic and packed in BPA-free cans.

Shopping List
Leafy greens (2-3 types)
Avocados
Sweet potatoes/yams
Onions
Garlic
Lemons
Riced cauliflower
Wild-caught seafood
Pastured or Omega-3 eggs
Compliant cheese
Canned wild-caught salmon
Olives
Millet
Nuts
Extra virgin olive oil
Vinegar
Coconut aminos

Stock Up

Keep this collection of ingredients on hand to ensure you can quickly put together a compliant meal.

WHERE TO FIND COMPLIANT FOODS

Depending on where you live you may struggle to find PP compliant foods. If you live near a Costco or Trader Joe's, however, you will find it easy to stock up. Not every store carries the same items, but this list of what others have found may help you decide whether a special trip is worth it. Amazon.com and Thrivemarket.com are also well-regarded sources. Fully pastured chicken is very hard to find. You can buy it online from Buy Ranch Direct, Circle C Farm, or Rainbow Ranch Farms.

Costco

CHEESE
Buffalo mozzarella
French Brie
Goat cheese
Gruyere
Manchego
Parmigiano Reggiano
Pecorino-Romano

MILK
A2 milk
Almond milk
Coconut milk (canned)

FLOUR, SWEETENERS
Almond flour
Birch Benders pancake mix
Lakanto monkfruit sweetener
Swerve

MEAT/SEAFOOD/PROTEIN
Canned sardines in olive oil
Eggs – pastured & Omega-3
Prosciutto di Parma
Teton Waters Grass-fed Sausages
Wild-caught canned salmon & tuna
Wild-caught seafood

OIL, VINEGAR, & SEASONINGS
Avocado oil
Avocado oil cooking spray
Avocado mayonnaise
Balsamic vinegar
Coconut aminos
Coconut oil
MCT oil
Olive oil
Sesame oil

PRODUCE
Avocados
Basil pesto
Frozen avocado chunks
Frozen organic cauliflower rice
Organic olives, black (canned)
Organic olives, green (water-packed)
Organic vegetables, fresh & frozen
Wholly Guacamole
Wildbrine Raw Organic Sauerkraut

NUTS, SEEDS
Hemp seeds
Macadamia nuts
Marcona almonds
Pecans
Pistachios
Walnuts

Trader Joe's

CHEESE
Asiago
Feta
French Fromage sliced cheese
Goat cheese (many varieties)
Gruyere
Manchego
Mini Petit Basque
Parmigiano-Reggiano
Triple crème brie

MILK/YOGURT/BUTTER
Almond milk
Coconut milk, coconut cream
Coconut yogurt
French Butter (Trader Jacques)
Ghee
Goat yogurt

FLOUR, SWEETENERS
Almond Flour
Organic liquid stevia

MEAT/SEAFOOD/PROTEIN
Canned sardines in olive oil
Chomps beef sticks
Eggs – Omega-3
Grass-fed/finished beef
Grass-fed/finished lamb
Prosciutto di Parma
Wild-caught canned crab
Wild-caught canned salmon & tuna
Wild-caught seafood, frozen

OIL, VINEGAR, & SEASONINGS
Avocado oil
Balsamic vinegar
Coconut aminos
Coconut oil
MCT oil
Nutritional yeast
Olive oil

RICE & PASTA
Basmati rice from India
Cauliflower gnocchi (frozen)

PRODUCE
Avocados (organic)
Beet chips
Fresh sliced jicama sticks
Frozen artichoke hearts
Lemons and limes (organic)
Jackfruit (canned)
Okra chips
Organic coconut
Organic vegetables, fresh & frozen
Parsnip chips
Riced veggies, fresh & frozen
Spiralized veggies, fresh & frozen

NUTS, SEEDS
Almonds
Flax seeds
Hazelnuts
Hemp seeds
Macadamia nuts
Pecans
Pistachios
Walnuts

WEEK 1

WEEKLY MEAL PLANNER

	BREAKFAST	LUNCH
Monday		
Tuesday		
Wednesday		
Thursday		
Friday		
Saturday		
Sunday		

WEEK OF:_____

DINNER	SNACKS

Shopping List

Store: Farmers Market

- ☐ Apples
- ☐ Veg to saute
- ☐ Veg to grill
- ☐ Veg to microwave

Store:

NOTES

WEEK 2

WEEKLY MEAL PLANNER

	BREAKFAST	LUNCH
Monday		
Tuesday		
Wednesday		
Thursday		
Friday		
Saturday		
Sunday		

WEEK OF:_____

DINNER	SNACKS

Shopping List

Store:

Store:

NOTES

WEEK 3

WEEKLY MEAL PLANNER

	BREAKFAST	LUNCH
Monday		
Tuesday		
Wednesday		
Thursday		
Friday		
Saturday		
Sunday		

WEEK OF:_____

DINNER	SNACKS

Shopping List

Store:

Store:

NOTES

WEEK 4

WEEKLY MEAL PLANNER

	BREAKFAST	LUNCH
Monday		
Tuesday		
Wednesday		
Thursday		
Friday		
Saturday		
Sunday		

WEEK OF:_____

DINNER	SNACKS

Shopping List

Store:

Store:

NOTES

WEEK 5

WEEKLY MEAL PLANNER

	BREAKFAST	LUNCH
Monday		
Tuesday		
Wednesday		
Thursday		
Friday		
Saturday		
Sunday		

WEEK OF:_____

DINNER	SNACKS

Shopping List

Store:

Store:

NOTES

WEEK 6

WEEKLY MEAL PLANNER

	BREAKFAST	LUNCH
Monday		
Tuesday		
Wednesday		
Thursday		
Friday		
Saturday		
Sunday		

WEEK OF:_____

DINNER	SNACKS

Shopping List

Store:

Store:

NOTES

WEEK 7

WEEKLY MEAL PLANNER

	BREAKFAST	LUNCH
Monday		
Tuesday		
Wednesday		
Thursday		
Friday		
Saturday		
Sunday		

WEEK OF:_____

DINNER	SNACKS

Shopping List

Store:

Store:

NOTES

WEEK 8

WEEKLY MEAL PLANNER

	BREAKFAST	LUNCH
Monday		
Tuesday		
Wednesday		
Thursday		
Friday		
Saturday		
Sunday		

WEEK OF:_____

DINNER	SNACKS

Shopping List

Store:

Store:

NOTES

WEEK 9

WEEKLY MEAL PLANNER

	BREAKFAST	LUNCH
Monday		
Tuesday		
Wednesday		
Thursday		
Friday		
Saturday		
Sunday		

WEEK OF:_____

DINNER	SNACKS

Shopping List

Store:

Store:

NOTES

WEEK 10

WEEKLY MEAL PLANNER

	BREAKFAST	LUNCH
Monday		
Tuesday		
Wednesday		
Thursday		
Friday		
Saturday		
Sunday		

WEEK OF:_____

DINNER	SNACKS

Shopping List

Store:
_____
_____
_____
_____
_____
_____
_____
_____
_____
_____
_____
_____

Store:
_____
_____
_____
_____
_____
_____
_____

NOTES

WEEK 11

WEEKLY MEAL PLANNER

	BREAKFAST	LUNCH
Monday		
Tuesday		
Wednesday		
Thursday		
Friday		
Saturday		
Sunday		

WEEK OF:_____

DINNER	SNACKS

Shopping List

Store:

Store:

NOTES

WEEK 12

WEEKLY MEAL PLANNER

	BREAKFAST	LUNCH
Monday		
Tuesday		
Wednesday		
Thursday		
Friday		
Saturday		
Sunday		

WEEK OF:_____

DINNER	SNACKS

Shopping List

Store:

Store:

NOTES

WEEK 13

WEEKLY MEAL PLANNER

	BREAKFAST	LUNCH
Monday		
Tuesday		
Wednesday		
Thursday		
Friday		
Saturday		
Sunday		

WEEK OF:_____

DINNER	SNACKS

Shopping List

Store:

Store:

WEEK 14

WEEKLY MEAL PLANNER

	BREAKFAST	LUNCH
Monday		
Tuesday		
Wednesday		
Thursday		
Friday		
Saturday		
Sunday		

WEEK OF:_____

DINNER	SNACKS

Shopping List

Store:

Store:

WEEK 15

WEEKLY MEAL PLANNER

	BREAKFAST	LUNCH
Monday		
Tuesday		
Wednesday		
Thursday		
Friday		
Saturday		
Sunday		

WEEK OF:_____

DINNER	SNACKS

Shopping List

Store:

Store:

NOTES

WEEK 16

WEEKLY MEAL PLANNER

	BREAKFAST	LUNCH
Monday		
Tuesday		
Wednesday		
Thursday		
Friday		
Saturday		
Sunday		

WEEK OF:_____

DINNER	SNACKS

Shopping List

Store:

Store:

NOTES

WEEK 17

WEEKLY MEAL PLANNER

	BREAKFAST	LUNCH
Monday		
Tuesday		
Wednesday		
Thursday		
Friday		
Saturday		
Sunday		

WEEK OF:_____

DINNER	SNACKS

Shopping List

Store:

Store:

NOTES

WEEK 18

WEEKLY MEAL PLANNER

	BREAKFAST	LUNCH
Monday		
Tuesday		
Wednesday		
Thursday		
Friday		
Saturday		
Sunday		

WEEK OF:_____

DINNER	SNACKS

Shopping List

Store:

Store:

WEEK 19

WEEKLY MEAL PLANNER

	BREAKFAST	LUNCH
Monday		
Tuesday		
Wednesday		
Thursday		
Friday		
Saturday		
Sunday		

WEEK OF:_____

DINNER	SNACKS

Shopping List

Store:

Store:

WEEK 20

WEEKLY MEAL PLANNER

	BREAKFAST	LUNCH
Monday		
Tuesday		
Wednesday		
Thursday		
Friday		
Saturday		
Sunday		

WEEK OF:_____

DINNER	SNACKS

Shopping List

Store:

Store:

NOTES

WEEK 21

WEEKLY MEAL PLANNER

	BREAKFAST	LUNCH
Monday		
Tuesday		
Wednesday		
Thursday		
Friday		
Saturday		
Sunday		

WEEK OF:_____

DINNER	SNACKS

Shopping List

Store:

Store:

NOTES

WEEK 22

WEEKLY MEAL PLANNER

	BREAKFAST	LUNCH
Monday		
Tuesday		
Wednesday		
Thursday		
Friday		
Saturday		
Sunday		

WEEK OF:_____

DINNER	SNACKS

Shopping List

Store:

Store:

NOTES

WEEK 23

WEEKLY MEAL PLANNER

	BREAKFAST	LUNCH
Monday		
Tuesday		
Wednesday		
Thursday		
Friday		
Saturday		
Sunday		

WEEK OF:_____

DINNER	SNACKS

Shopping List

Store:

Store:

NOTES

WEEK 24

WEEKLY MEAL PLANNER

	BREAKFAST	LUNCH
Monday		
Tuesday		
Wednesday		
Thursday		
Friday		
Saturday		
Sunday		

WEEK OF:_____

DINNER	SNACKS

Shopping List

Store:

Store:

NOTES

WEEK 25

WEEKLY MEAL PLANNER

	BREAKFAST	LUNCH
Monday		
Tuesday		
Wednesday		
Thursday		
Friday		
Saturday		
Sunday		

WEEK OF:_____

DINNER	SNACKS

Shopping List

Store:

Store:

NOTES

WEEK 26

WEEKLY MEAL PLANNER

	BREAKFAST	LUNCH
Monday		
Tuesday		
Wednesday		
Thursday		
Friday		
Saturday		
Sunday		

WEEK OF:_____

DINNER	SNACKS

Shopping List

Store:

_____
_____
_____
_____
_____
_____
_____
_____
_____
_____
_____

Store:

_____
_____
_____
_____
_____
_____

NOTES

WEEK 27

WEEKLY MEAL PLANNER

	BREAKFAST	LUNCH
Monday		
Tuesday		
Wednesday		
Thursday		
Friday		
Saturday		
Sunday		

WEEK OF:_____

DINNER	SNACKS

Shopping List

Store:

_____
_____
_____
_____
_____
_____
_____
_____
_____
_____
_____

Store:

_____
_____
_____
_____
_____
_____
_____

NOTES

WEEK 28

WEEKLY MEAL PLANNER

	BREAKFAST	LUNCH
Monday		
Tuesday		
Wednesday		
Thursday		
Friday		
Saturday		
Sunday		

WEEK OF:_____

DINNER	SNACKS

Shopping List

Store:

Store:

NOTES

WEEK 29

WEEKLY MEAL PLANNER

	BREAKFAST	LUNCH
Monday		
Tuesday		
Wednesday		
Thursday		
Friday		
Saturday		
Sunday		

WEEK OF:_____

DINNER	SNACKS

Shopping List

Store:

_____
_____
_____
_____
_____
_____
_____
_____
_____
_____

Store:

_____
_____
_____
_____
_____
_____
_____
_____

NOTES

WEEK 30

WEEKLY MEAL PLANNER

	BREAKFAST	LUNCH
Monday		
Tuesday		
Wednesday		
Thursday		
Friday		
Saturday		
Sunday		

WEEK OF:_____

DINNER	SNACKS

Shopping List

Store:
_____
_____
_____
_____
_____
_____
_____
_____
_____
_____
_____

Store:
_____
_____
_____
_____
_____
_____
_____
_____

NOTES

WEEK 31

WEEKLY MEAL PLANNER

	BREAKFAST	LUNCH
Monday		
Tuesday		
Wednesday		
Thursday		
Friday		
Saturday		
Sunday		

WEEK OF:_____

DINNER	SNACKS

Shopping List

Store:

Store:

NOTES

WEEK 32

WEEKLY MEAL PLANNER

	BREAKFAST	LUNCH
Monday		
Tuesday		
Wednesday		
Thursday		
Friday		
Saturday		
Sunday		

WEEK OF:_____

DINNER	SNACKS

Shopping List

Store:
_____
_____
_____
_____
_____
_____
_____
_____
_____
_____
_____
_____

Store:
_____
_____
_____
_____
_____
_____
_____
_____
_____

NOTES

WEEK 33

WEEKLY MEAL PLANNER

	BREAKFAST	LUNCH
Monday		
Tuesday		
Wednesday		
Thursday		
Friday		
Saturday		
Sunday		

WEEK OF:_____

DINNER	SNACKS

Shopping List

Store:

Store:

WEEK 34

WEEKLY MEAL PLANNER

	BREAKFAST	LUNCH
Monday		
Tuesday		
Wednesday		
Thursday		
Friday		
Saturday		
Sunday		

WEEK OF:_____

DINNER	SNACKS

Shopping List

Store:

Store:

NOTES

WEEK 35

WEEKLY MEAL PLANNER

	BREAKFAST	LUNCH
Monday		
Tuesday		
Wednesday		
Thursday		
Friday		
Saturday		
Sunday		

WEEK OF:_____

DINNER	SNACKS

Shopping List

Store:

_____

Store:

_____

NOTES

WEEK 36

WEEKLY MEAL PLANNER

	BREAKFAST	LUNCH
Monday		
Tuesday		
Wednesday		
Thursday		
Friday		
Saturday		
Sunday		

WEEK OF:_____

DINNER	SNACKS

Shopping List

Store:

_____
_____
_____
_____
_____
_____
_____
_____
_____
_____

Store:

_____
_____
_____
_____
_____
_____
_____
_____

NOTES

WEEK 37

WEEKLY MEAL PLANNER

	BREAKFAST	LUNCH
Monday		
Tuesday		
Wednesday		
Thursday		
Friday		
Saturday		
Sunday		

WEEK OF:_____

DINNER	SNACKS

Shopping List

Store:

Store:

NOTES

WEEK 38

WEEKLY MEAL PLANNER

	BREAKFAST	LUNCH
Monday		
Tuesday		
Wednesday		
Thursday		
Friday		
Saturday		
Sunday		

WEEK OF:_____

DINNER	SNACKS

Shopping List

Store:

Store:

NOTES

WEEK 39

WEEKLY MEAL PLANNER

	BREAKFAST	LUNCH
Monday		
Tuesday		
Wednesday		
Thursday		
Friday		
Saturday		
Sunday		

WEEK OF:_____

DINNER	SNACKS

Shopping List

Store:

Store:

NOTES

WEEK 40

WEEKLY MEAL PLANNER

	BREAKFAST	LUNCH
Monday		
Tuesday		
Wednesday		
Thursday		
Friday		
Saturday		
Sunday		

WEEK OF:_____

DINNER	SNACKS

Shopping List

Store:

Store:

NOTES

WEEK 41

WEEKLY MEAL PLANNER

	BREAKFAST	LUNCH
Monday		
Tuesday		
Wednesday		
Thursday		
Friday		
Saturday		
Sunday		

WEEK OF:_____

DINNER	SNACKS

Shopping List

Store:

Store:

NOTES

WEEK 42

WEEKLY MEAL PLANNER

	BREAKFAST	LUNCH
Monday		
Tuesday		
Wednesday		
Thursday		
Friday		
Saturday		
Sunday		

WEEK OF:_____

DINNER	SNACKS

Shopping List

Store:

_____
_____
_____
_____
_____
_____
_____
_____
_____
_____
_____

Store:

_____
_____
_____
_____
_____
_____
_____
_____

WEEK 43

WEEKLY MEAL PLANNER

	BREAKFAST	LUNCH
Monday		
Tuesday		
Wednesday		
Thursday		
Friday		
Saturday		
Sunday		

WEEK OF:_____

DINNER	SNACKS

Shopping List

Store:

Store:

NOTES

WEEK 44

WEEKLY MEAL PLANNER

	BREAKFAST	LUNCH
Monday		
Tuesday		
Wednesday		
Thursday		
Friday		
Saturday		
Sunday		

WEEK OF:_____

DINNER	SNACKS

Shopping List

Store:

Store:

NOTES

WEEK 45

WEEKLY MEAL PLANNER

	BREAKFAST	LUNCH
Monday		
Tuesday		
Wednesday		
Thursday		
Friday		
Saturday		
Sunday		

WEEK OF:_____

DINNER	SNACKS

Shopping List

Store:

Store:

NOTES

WEEK 46

WEEKLY MEAL PLANNER

	BREAKFAST	LUNCH
Monday		
Tuesday		
Wednesday		
Thursday		
Friday		
Saturday		
Sunday		

WEEK OF:_____

DINNER	SNACKS

Shopping List

Store:

Store:

NOTES

WEEK 47

WEEKLY MEAL PLANNER

	BREAKFAST	LUNCH
Monday		
Tuesday		
Wednesday		
Thursday		
Friday		
Saturday		
Sunday		

WEEK OF:_____

DINNER	SNACKS

Shopping List

Store:

Store:

NOTES

WEEK 48

WEEKLY MEAL PLANNER

	BREAKFAST	LUNCH
Monday		
Tuesday		
Wednesday		
Thursday		
Friday		
Saturday		
Sunday		

WEEK OF:_____

DINNER	SNACKS

Shopping List

Store:
_____
_____
_____
_____
_____
_____
_____
_____
_____
_____
_____

Store:
_____
_____
_____
_____
_____
_____
_____

NOTES

WEEK 49

WEEKLY MEAL PLANNER

	BREAKFAST	LUNCH
Monday		
Tuesday		
Wednesday		
Thursday		
Friday		
Saturday		
Sunday		

WEEK OF:_____

DINNER	SNACKS

Shopping List

Store:

_____
_____
_____
_____
_____
_____
_____
_____
_____
_____
_____
_____

Store:

_____
_____
_____
_____
_____
_____
_____
_____
_____
_____

NOTES

A Christmas Party

- Mistletoe margatinis — virgin Never Been Kissed
    elderflower & cranberry

WEEK 50

WEEKLY MEAL PLANNER

	BREAKFAST	LUNCH
Monday		
Tuesday		
Wednesday		
Thursday		
Friday		
Saturday		
Sunday		

WEEK OF:_____

DINNER	SNACKS

Shopping List

Store:

Store:

NOTES

WEEK 51

WEEKLY MEAL PLANNER

	BREAKFAST	LUNCH
Monday		
Tuesday		
Wednesday		
Thursday		
Friday		
Saturday		
Sunday		

WEEK OF:_____

DINNER	SNACKS

Shopping List

Store:

_____
_____
_____
_____
_____
_____
_____
_____
_____
_____
_____
_____

Store:

_____
_____
_____
_____
_____
_____
_____
_____

WEEK 52

WEEKLY MEAL PLANNER

	BREAKFAST	LUNCH
Monday		
Tuesday		
Wednesday		
Thursday		
Friday		
Saturday		
Sunday		

WEEK OF:_____

DINNER	SNACKS

Shopping List

Store:

_____
_____
_____
_____
_____
_____
_____
_____
_____
_____
_____
_____

Store:

_____
_____
_____
_____
_____
_____
_____

NOTES

Made in the USA
Las Vegas, NV
11 December 2020